NO PLACE LIKE DOME!!
A Syracuse and National Cartoon Retrospective
by Joe Glisson

To Denny! With all my best wishes!!
— Glisson, 2012

©2012 Joe Glisson Productions. All rights reserved.
www.joeglisson.com

THIS IS JUST THE BEGINNING!

You can find Joe Glisson's latest cartoons every week in the *Syracuse New Times*, Central New York's alternative newsweekly.

Free every Wednesday at more than 1,050 outlets throughout Central New York. Mail subscriptions available for $39.95. Call (315) 422-7011.

www.syracusenewtimes.com

Dedication

With Much Respect To
Murray Tinkelman

Artist, Teacher, Photographer, Author, Historian,
Mentor, Friend, and National Treasure...
The Cross-Hatch Kid.

Foreword

For so many of us who have bundled ourselves to journey across campus on a cold Winter's night or spent a late Summer evening wondering 'why didn't air conditioning come with that naming rights deal'... The Dome has a special place in our hearts. While many have written eloquently on the stars and games under the Teflon tent in the corner of my beautiful alma mater, there is just something special about a cartoon. Growing up in New York City I remember opening the sports pages of the Daily News to see the cartoons which captured the story of the day. It takes a special person to in one scene, with few if any words, add perspective and capture the mood of an entire fan base. Game after game, season after season, Joe Glisson has done just that. His creativity and talent have left a collection to remember younger days, sad days and glory days. For those of us who have shed an Orange tinged tear or have a memory of a magic moment from a 'Cuse classic, we treasure this collection of Joe's talents. It truly does remind us that "There's No Place Like Dome!"

—Mike Tirico
ABC & ESPN Sports

Tough To Get A Big Head In This Town

Coach P's Problems Start

Trying To Get In The Dance With 18 Wins

Still Trying

Didn't Make The NCAA's

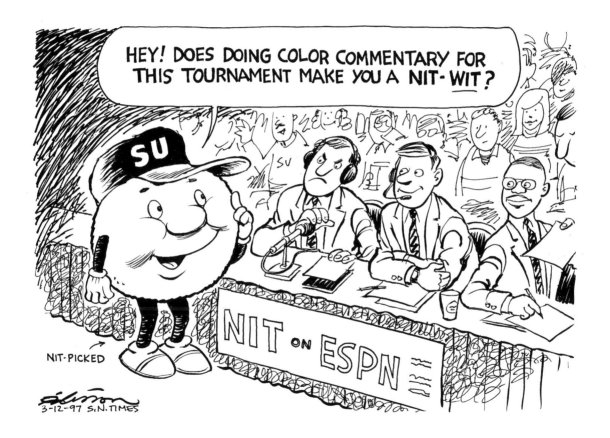

Miami's Mascot Ruffles H.O.F. Dolph's Feathers

Roy Simmons, Jr. Knows How To Get There

Players Have To Learn X's And O's

McNabb Barfs On National TV

That Sinking Feeling Starts Early

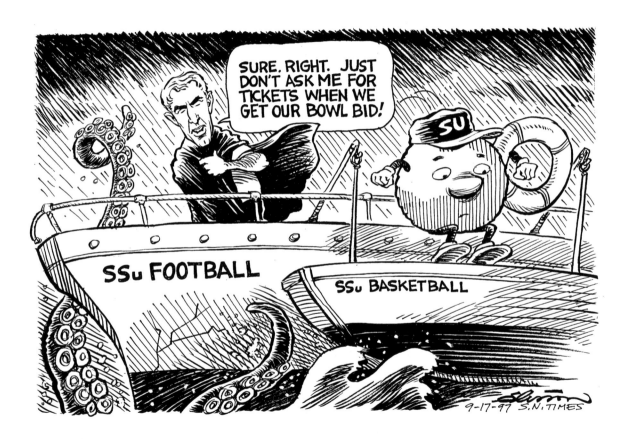

Marathon Is Always Pre-Season Opponent

The Future Looks Bleak Without Him

Winning Flutie Gets Own Cereal

The Powell Dynasty Continues

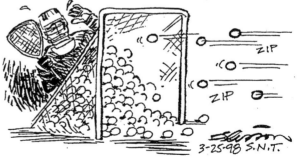

Roy Simmons Retires

University Tries To Reward Fans

Mark McGwire Needs A Maris Asterisk

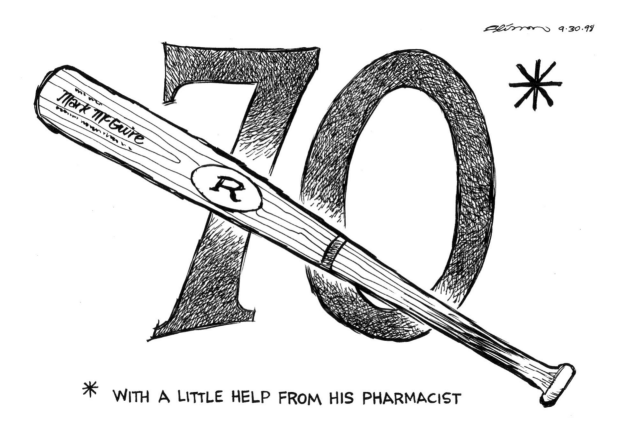

* WITH A LITTLE HELP FROM HIS PHARMACIST

California Angels Owner Dies

Going Bowling

John Thompson Retires

Brandi Chastain Pulls Off Her Jersey

McNabb Earns Big Payday

Donovan Leaves Big Shoes To Fill

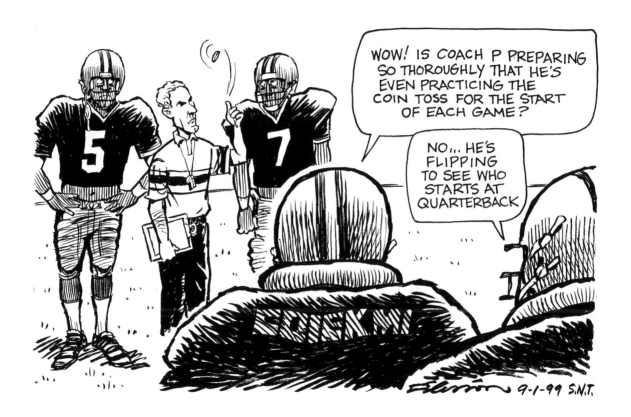

Defense Not Our Strong Suit

Lax Team Keeps Repeating Itself

Tiger Woods On Top Of The World

With Losses, The Calls For His Head Begin

Rough Year For Both Of Us

University Drops Wrestling

Jim Sets Mark Near St. Pat's Day

Fishing Tournament Has Million Dollar Prize

Who Wants To Be A Millionaire?

Still Looking For The Right Fit

Olympic Scoring Hard To Understand

WITH THE WAY THE JUDGES VOTE, THEY SHOULD CALL IT **GO FIGURE!** SKATING

Hoping For Invite To NCAA's

NCAA Take Women, Not Men, In Tourney

Players And Fans Show Unity With Stubble

SU Lax Playing Great In NCAA's

Baseball Is Contemplating A Strike

Going Down The Drain

Otto Talks Trash

Crunch Looking Good

Just To Make It Interesting

Have To Beat Longhorns To Make Final Four

National Champions

#1 Team Visits The White House

Local Thoroughbred In Kentucky Derby

A Fish Story

The Football Team's Not Well

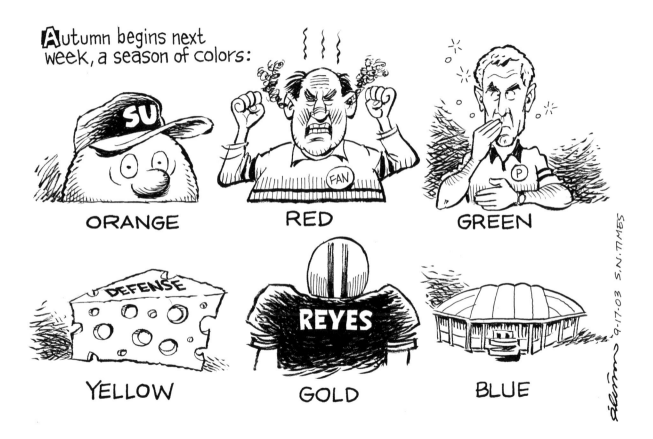

Terminator Speaks From Experience

"P" Courts The New Chancellor

Fair Is Fair

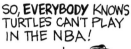

Looking For That Knockout Punch

Dream On

Angry Football Fans Want Pasqualoni Gone

Boston Wins Series To Break The "Curse"

Some Root For Coach P To Fail

Coach P Saved By The Bowl

You've Come A Long Way Baby

Pasqualoni & Crouthamel Out, The Dr. Is In

Happy Holidazed

Greg Robinson New Football Coach

The NHL Goes On Strike

Steinbrenner Isn't Happy

Apologies To Stan Lee

Armstrong Wins Another Tour De France

The University Tries To Make Its Mark

The Times Are A Changin'

Another Football Season To Begin

Another Opening Loss

Tie It You'll Like It

Our Favorite Teams Keep Losing

Robinson Needs A Quarterback

First Season Is Over

Bowled Over

Dome Has "Dress Like '70s Boeheim" Night

A Win Over Villanova Will Put Us In NCAA's

Team Finally Wakes Up

Barry Bonds Plays His Last Card

This Topic Just Won't Go Away

Fans Support While Waiting For Wins

New Paint Job, Same Old Ride

Enjoy It Now, It Won't Last

Bad Start Doesn't Look To Get Better

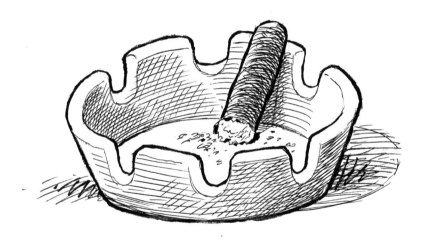

SU Sports Has It's Ups And Downs

Blue Christmas

91

Same Old, Same Old

Basketball Program Has Infractions

When Sports Injuries Are Used In Real Life

Yanks Take Chance On Clemens

If Some Parents Had Their Way

NFL QB Arrested For Illegal Dog Fights

Robinson Tries To Find Right Pieces

SU Advertising Slogan Is Prophetic

Finally A Giant Killer Game

Now, Back To Reality

Coach Robinson Remains Optimistic

Latest CNY National Champs

It's Getting Out Of Hand

Orangewomen Break Into Top Rankings

Crunch Are In The Playoffs

Syracuse Lacrosse Back On Top

Boston Loses Ramirez To LA

Michael Phelps Wins 8 Olympic Medals

Robinson Feeling Pressure To Win

Things Look Grim This Fall

The Coach Is Spaced Out

Robinson Axed As Head Football Coach

Doug Marrone Named As New Coach

Pressure To Win Starts Early

Alex Rodriguez Latest Caught Shooting Up

SU Plays School Named Stephen Austin In NCAA's

Some Fans Will Never Appreciate Boeheim

SU Basketball Stars Elope To NBA

They Were Stars Together In High School

Coach Marrone Ready To Make His Mark

121

Entering Enemy Territory

Syracuse Fans Are Often Bi-Polar

Turning Stone Tournament Stuck With Fall Weather

Team's Not Afraid Of Top-Ranked Bearcats

Marrone Deals With Injuries And No Depth

Senior QB Paulus Showed Team How To Win

Pre-Conference Play Gets High Marks

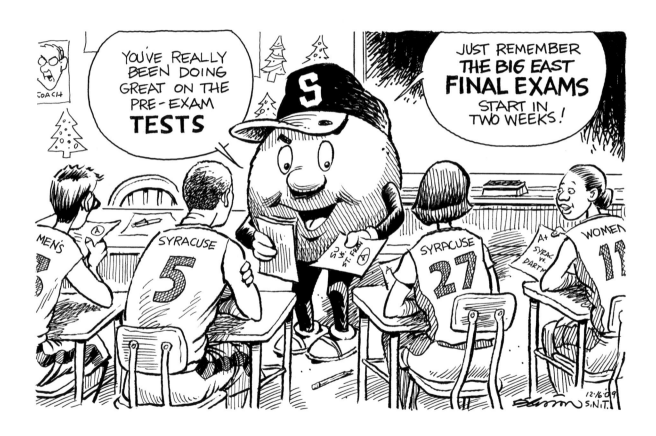

Everybody's Gunning For League Leader

Coach Mac's Grandson Signs With Orange

Both Teams Currently Number One In Nation

Arinze Blows Out Knee Before NCAA Tournament

The Media Loves Even Sub-Par Tiger Woods

Syracuse Hall Of Famer Un-Plugged

Pitching Sensation Leads To Sell-Out Crowds

World Cup Bans Plastic Rally Horns At Games

Steinbrenner Takes His Final Road Trip

After Years Of Rejection...

Some Fans Still Not Sure About New Coach

Syracuse Celebrates 30 Years in Carrier Dome

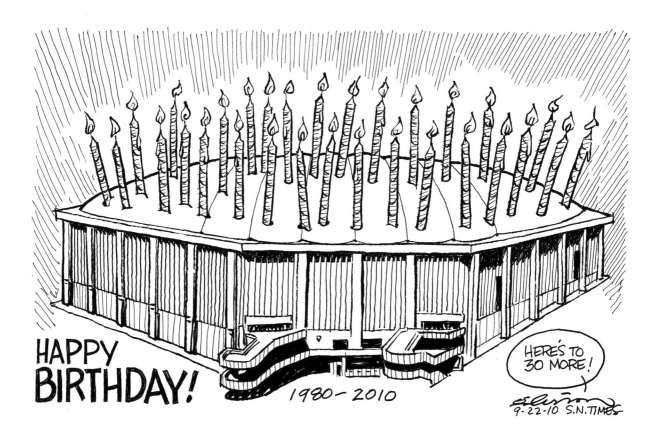

The Football Team Has Good Start This Year

Season Is A Work Of Art So Far

SU Beats W. Virginia And Ben's Ghost Appears

We Win The Pinstripe Bowl At Yankee Stadium

144

Harriers Have A Dynasty Going

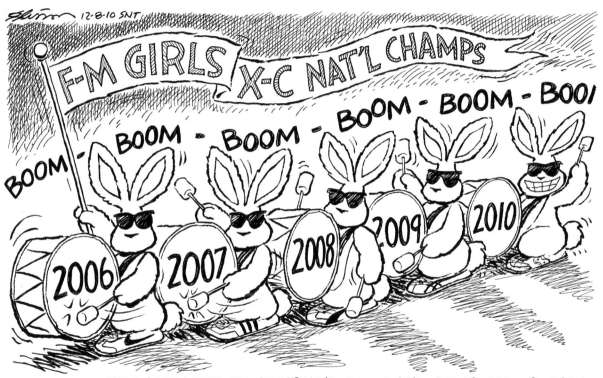

SU Punter Has Brain Tumor Removed

146

Every Game's Hard Fought In The Big East

Revenge On West Point For Last Year's Upset

Carmelo Anthony Is Traded To The Knicks

Syracuse Pulls Plug On Swim Program

Odds Aren't Good For Post-Season Play

If Steinbrenner Wasn't Dead This Would Kill Him

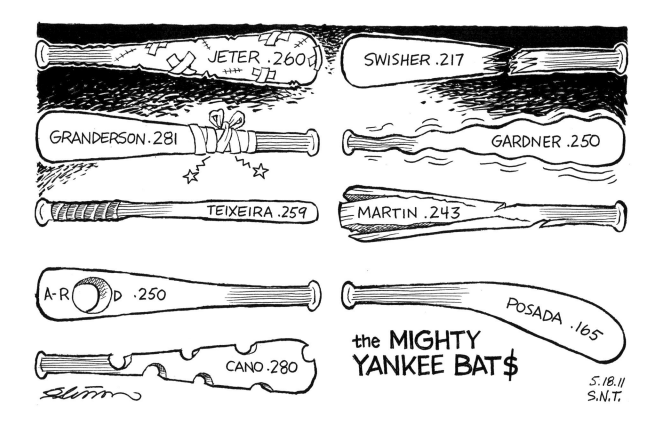

Hall-Of-Famer Takes University Position

Tiger Woods Toothless In Tournaments

SU Plays A Rare Thursday Night Game

Leaving Home

Coach Whines Over Bad Call

157

'Cuse And Buffalo Both Fall From First Place

SU Destroys Top-Ranked West Virginia

Sex Scandal Hits Close To Home

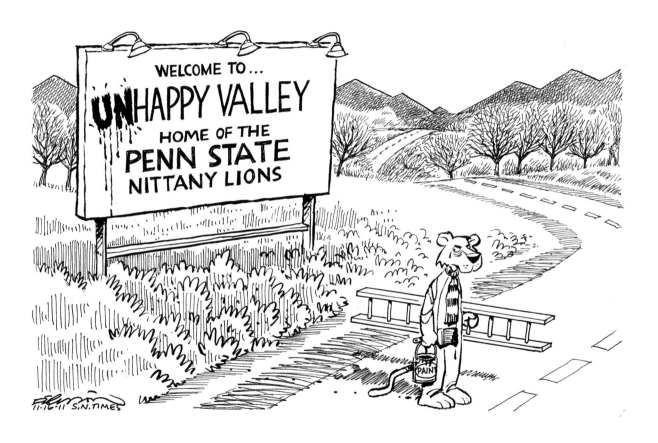

Sex Scandal Hits Closer To Home

New Year Brings New Hope

Leap Year: Jim Moves Past Rupp For Wins

Fab Melo Is Out Of Action

165

Big East Champions

Almost A Storybook Ending

Tully's
Great Food & Good Times

Proud Supporter of Syracuse Sports

 Join our Email Club for special

 Like us!

Follow us!

www.tullysgoodtimes.com